613.81 q £11 05

STRAIGHT TALKING ABOUT DRUGS

Alcohol

Sean Connolly

D1349272

W
FRANKLIN WATTS
LONDON•SYDNEY

An Appleseed Editions book

First published in 2006 by Franklin Watts
338 Euston Road, London NW1 3BH

Franklin Watts Australia
Hachette Children's Books
Level 17/207 Kent St, Sydney, NSW 2000

© 2006 Appleseed Editions

Created by Appleseed Editions Ltd,
Well House, Friars Hill, Guestling,
East Sussex TN35 4ET

Designed by Guy Callaby
Edited by Pip Morgan
Artwork by Karen Donnelly
Picture research by Cathy Tatge

ISBN 0 7496 6754 0

Dewey Classification: 362.292

A CIP catalogue for this book is available from
the British Library.

Photograph acknowledgements
Photographs by Alamy (Boyd, Directphoto.org, Juliet Ferguson,
Medical-on-line, Eric Nathan, Woodystock), Guy Callaby, Getty
Images (AHMAD AL-RUBAYE / AFP, Daniel Allen, ODD ANDERSON /
AFP, Bruce Ayres, Jon Bradley, Lauren Burke, Matt ardy, Philip
Condit II, Christopher Furlong, Philip Lee Harvey, PHILIPPE HUGUEN
/ AFP, The Images Bank, Library of Congress, MAXIM MARMUR /
AFP, Fran May, David McNew / Newsmakers, Erin Patrice O'Brien,
Frank Siteman, Henrik Sorensen, Justin Sullivan, Mario Tama,
Brunno Vincent, Carsten Witte, David Woolley, David Young-Wolff)
Front cover photograph by Getty Images (Jon Bradley)

Printed in China

Contents

Alcohol is an important part of many people's lives, particularly at parties and other social events.

"What's the buzz?"... "Where's the buzz?"... "I'm buzzing". These comments are all linked to alcohol and help to give it an exciting feel – especially for young people. Like other forbidden activities, drinking alcohol is something that some people like to talk about secretly, or to boast about to their friends or others at school.

Part of a cool crowd

It is not hard to see how you might be tempted to try something, such as beer, wine or an alcopop, that seems to offer a chance for excitement and wild times – the buzz that many people talk about when describing a lively party or some crazy prank.

Some use the word buzz to describe the sensation inside their head when they feel the effects of alcohol or some other drug. To feel the buzz, to be part of it, to sense it around you – these make you want to do something. The downside, especially for young people, is that by not taking part, they will be outsiders or not part of a cool crowd.

> **Kids who drink are more likely to be victims of violent crime, to be involved in alcohol-related traffic accidents, and to have serious school-related problems.** "

From the Introduction to *Make a Difference: Talk to Your Child About Alcohol*, produced by the US National Institute on Alcohol Abuse and Alcoholism.

Use and abuse

People in most parts of the world accept that alcohol can play a part in social events, such as weddings and parties. Few would find anything wrong with using alcohol in this way. Problems only develop when people abuse it: they drink too much or too often or when they don't really need it. Then it can become a danger – both to the drinker and to those around them.

Learning to distinguish between use and abuse is an important part of growing up. The results of drinking too much alcohol can be serious, even fatal, but people can learn how to avoid them.

Riot police stand prepared at a European football match. Sporting rivalries can turn ugly and violent when supporters drink too much.

Alcohol is a drug that can change your mood. It is one of the most common mood-changing drugs in the world. Unlike other drugs, such as cannabis or cocaine, it is legal in most countries, even if there are laws to say who can or cannot drink it.

Part of our culture

People have been producing wine, beer and other alcoholic drinks for thousands of years. As a result, alcohol has become part of the culture in many countries, almost a way of life: for example, the English drink beer, the Scottish drink whisky, the French and Italians drink wine, the Russians drink vodka

Alcoholic drinks can be part of the graveside offerings during Mexico's annual Day of the Dead on 1–2 November.

and the Japanese drink sake, which is wine made from rice.

Alcohol even plays a part in many religions. Bread and wine are used in many Christian services. Mexicans leave bottles of tequila and beer by the graves of loved ones each year during the Day of the Dead.

An everyday chemical

Most people use the word alcohol to refer to the mood-changing ingredient in beer, wine and other alcoholic drinks. The alcohol in drinks is ethyl alcohol (ethanol is another name). Ethyl alcohol is produced naturally in a process called fermentation, when sugar is turned into alcohol using yeast. Beer and wine are produced by fermentation and the alcohol they contain has a concentration of up to about 15 per cent ABV (alcohol by volume). In other words, up to 15 per cent of the liquid in these drinks is ethyl alcohol.

A process called distillation can increase this concentration. Rum, gin, whisky and vodka – all produced by distillation – have concentrations of about 40–45 per cent ABV, and sometimes even more.

Ethyl alcohol is only one of a larger group of chemical compounds, all called alcohols, which are used to make varnish, ink, soap, antifreeze, and even explosives. Most are poisonous for humans.

Customers at pubs and off-licences can choose from many different alcoholic drinks, which vary widely in alcoholic strength.

A drawing from the Middle Ages shows people gathering and crushing grapes, and collecting the finished wine in a jug.

Drink through the ages

Wine is probably the oldest alcoholic drink. It is made from grapes, which are are native to the Middle East. The first evidence of people growing grapes to make wine – as opposed to finding wine accidentally – comes from the Caucasus region (where Georgia and Armenia are today). Vineyards almost certainly existed there between 6,000 and 8,000 years ago.

We know that labourers working on the Egyptian pyramids drank beer and that Egyptian religious ceremonies included wine. By about 500 BC the ancient Greeks were producing enough wine to ship to other countries. The Romans followed their example and grew grapes in vineyards throughout their empire, including the modern wine-producing regions of France, Spain and Italy.

The Arabs were the first people to produce stronger alcoholic drinks using distillation, probably in the 10th century AD. Europeans were quick to adopt this process. The word alcohol comes from an Arabic word meaning powder, a substance sometimes mixed with distilled alcoholic drinks.

Wine and beer were especially popular with Europeans throughout the Middle Ages, partly because distilled drinks such as whisky and rum were expensive to produce.

In the 18th century, new techniques made some distilled drinks, especially gin, much cheaper. This caused alarm in London and other major cities. Londoners could get "drunk for a penny and dead drunk for tuppence (two pennies)". The British government added a tax to gin, making it more expensive and so less popular. Most governments continue to tax alcoholic drinks – partly to raise money and partly to discourage excessive drinking.

Measuring alcohol
It is important to know how strong alcoholic drinks are, so people can drink sensibly. This strength is usually shown on the label of bottles and cans of drinks, with a number followed by Alcohol % Vol or % Vol or % ABV. Alcohol experts use the term unit.

This list shows the strength of common alcoholic drinks:

Small glass of wine (9–11% ABV): **1 unit**

Half pint of ordinary strength beer/lager/cider (4% ABV): **1 unit**

25 ml pub measure of spirits, such as whisky or vodka, (40% ABV): **1 unit**

330 ml bottle of alcopop (5% ABV): **1.7 units**

The accepted sensible health limit for men is three to four units a day and two to three units a day for women.

This large bottle of lager is 710 ml, or about a pint and a quarter.

Many people find that alcohol makes them feel happier and less shy when they are socializing in a group.

Most people drink alcohol because they believe it will improve the way they feel. Usually they drink with others – at parties or in a group at a pub or someone's house. For these drinkers, alcohol plays an important part in breaking the ice – making them feel more relaxed and sociable. How relaxed people feel, or whether that feeling goes beyond just unwinding, depends on how much they have drunk. It also depends on other factors such as tiredness, how big they are and how much they ate before drinking (two factors that can slow the effects of alcohol).

People sometimes turn to alcohol because they feel it will make them happier, at least for a while. Lonely, unhappy or worried people can turn to drink and hit the bottle as a way of avoiding their concerns.

Chemical reaction

The changes alcohol triggers arise from chemical reactions inside the body. Alcohol passes into the bloodstream through the lining of the small intestine and then to other parts of the body, especially the brain. Alcohol changes the way the brain operates, especially the parts that control concentration, making judgements and body movements. The amount of change depends on how much alcohol reaches the brain.

People can find some of these changes pleasant. For example, after having a drink someone might feel more able to mingle with strangers at a party. Without alcohol the brain might have sent the message, "those people might not find me interesting". Alcohol changes

MORE DANGEROUS

The brain changes during adolescence, and alcohol can seriously harm its growth and development almost at once and also in the future. The frontal lobe (one of the largest regions of the brain), along with many nerve pathways and connections, continue to develop until the age of 16. The brain itself takes another four years to mature. Damage from alcohol at this stage can last a long time and the brain may never recover. Even moderate drinking affects learning and memory far more in young people than in adults.

the brain's way of making judgements – in this case, from being cautious in a group to being more sociable.

Fat and muscle tissue in the body absorb some alcohol before it reaches the brain, so heavy-set or muscular people are often less affected than a thinner person by the same amount of alcohol. Larger people – and most men, compared to women – also have more blood, which can dilute alcohol and lessen the effects of drink.

Many men like to drink large glasses of beer, ale or lager.

Binge drinkers get through a lot of alcohol – or drink very quickly – in order to feel the effects of being drunk.

BINGE DRINKING

People become very drunk when the alcohol in their blood – the blood alcohol level – increases before the body can deal with the alcohol already there. It takes several hours for the effects of a single drink (such as a beer or a glass of wine) to wear off, so having several drinks usually leads to drunkenness.

Most responsible drinkers pace themselves so this does not happen. Others deliberately drink large amounts over a short time to get drunk. Young people – even those old enough to drink legally – risk injuring themselves or others with this behaviour, which is called binge drinking. Alcohol awareness organizations are concerned that advertising aimed at young people makes drinking seem necessary for having a good time.

EFFECTS OF ALCOHOL

These are the progressive effects of becoming drunk (intoxication). People go through these stages if they continue drinking alcohol without allowing enough time for the effects to wear off.

Stage 1

People become more confident, comfortable and talkative.

Stage 2

Drinkers' thinking becomes less clear, and they will probably say things they are likely to regret later.

Stage 3

They become unsteady and confused, with slurred speech. They might behave unpredictably and become violent.

Stage 4

Drinkers are very confused and find it hard to stand up. At this stage, many drinkers pass out (become unconscious).

Stage 5

People who remain conscious and continue drinking at this stage are in grave danger. Their nervous system has trouble working, so they might stop breathing and even die.

During celebrations fuelled by alcohol, some students at Oxford University jump off the city's bridges into the river.

> **I don't particularly worry about the negative physical effects – not yet, anyway. In spite of the booze 'n' fags, I'm reasonably fit, and at my last check-up (five years ago, admittedly) my liver was fine. If I have a hangover headache, I'm fairly stoical about it. However, the psychological effects do worry me. I can take an aspirin for a sore head, but the only thing I can take for the anxiety and depression that follow a heavy bout of drinking is... another drink, of course.**

Joe, a UK musician and gardener living in Germany, discussing his drinking habits on a TV programme about alcohol.

SOBERING MYTHS

A number of myths surround the issue of drinking and sobering up afterwards. Many people believe that drinking coffee helps to speed up the sobering process because it contains the stimulant caffeine. Others say that taking a cold shower or walking it off can help someone become sober more quickly. None of these actions actually helps get rid of the effects of alcohol any quicker. The body does this at its own pace. Such misconceptions are risky if someone has drunk enough to be a dangerous driver. Alcohol also affects judgement, so a drinker can easily believe these myths and convince others that he or she is safe behind the wheel.

A sign beside a highway urges motorists to think carefully about drinking and driving.

Drinking alcohol, especially regularly over a long period, can have far more effects than simply making someone merry or even very drunk. Some effects are felt after the first time someone has drunk alcohol. Most regular drinkers can describe the awful feeling of a hangover (see page 18). Alcohol also works over a longer period and can lead to serious medical conditions if a person drinks a lot for several years or longer.

Going beyond the limit

All these effects arise because alcohol is a drug that affects the body. Too much of any drug can damage the body or the way it operates. That is why medicines have clear instructions on how much to take and what to do if someone has a bad reaction to it. Sensible drinkers know that alcohol also has safety limits. Going beyond these, especially time after time, is very dangerous.

As well as a headache, many people with hangovers have an upset stomach because alcohol affects the fluids in the stomach and digestive system. A hangover usually wears off after a few hours, although some drinkers have 'the hair of the dog' – another alcoholic drink to relieve the pain. That just postpones the hangover, which is usually worse when it does hit. Needing a drink in the morning is a sign that a person might be dependent on alcohol (see pages 20–23).

LONG-TERM EFFECTS

Alcohol reaches most parts of the body via the bloodstream. Getting drunk and feeling dry and sick because of a hangover are some of the short-term effects of having alcohol in the body. But regular drinking over time can have damaging – even fatal – consequences. Below are some parts of the body that can be affected by long-term drinking, no matter how young the drinker is.

1 Liver *The liver can only absorb alcohol slowly. Too much alcohol damages liver cells, leading to diseases such as cirrhosis and cancer.*

2 Stomach *Alcohol can make people very sick and can cause ulcers and other stomach problems.*

3 Heart *Alcohol can make the heart work much harder than normal. This overwork can lead to high blood pressure and heart disease.*

4 Brain *Alcohol kills brain cells and depresses the central nervous system. It has a bad effect on concentration, balance, co-ordination, reflexes, vision and judgement.*

> *I think that awareness of alcohol poisoning should be higher. I am a high honour student, with a part time job, I am smart. I got so drunk last month that I passed out up town, almost died and got taken by my friends to the hospital.*

Seventeen-year-old boy, quoted in New Brunswick Student Drug Use Survey 2002.

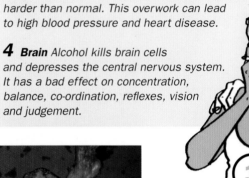

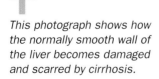

This photograph shows how the normally smooth wall of the liver becomes damaged and scarred by cirrhosis.

THE SOCIAL COST

Alcohol damages society as a whole, contributing to or causing a wide range of crimes. The Alcohol Concern website has gathered some alarming statistics from government reports and alcohol surveys in the UK. The facts and figures paint an alarming picture of the role of alcohol in society.

● *In 1999, there were 1.2 million reports of alcohol-related violence – about 22,000 each week.*

● *One in five violent crimes takes place in or around pubs and clubs – 70 per cent of these on weekend evenings.*

● *About one-third of violent incidents between partners took place when one of them had been drinking.*

● *In 2001 and 2002, 47 per cent of victims of violent crimes said that their attackers had been under the influence of alcohol at the time.*

THE MORNING AFTER

One of the first unpleasant side-effects of drinking alcohol is a hangover. Among other things, alcohol takes moisture from the body's cells, including the brain. This dryness leads to headaches and an uncomfortable reaction to sudden noises. People usually feel the effects of a hangover after the immediate effects of drinking alcohol have worn off, often when they wake up the next morning.

American police officers test the ability of a suspected drink-driver to walk in a straight line without losing his balance.

SEARCHING QUESTION

National health schemes or health insurance companies, such as those in the UK and Canada, pay for most expensive medical treatment. Some patients need treatment because they have drunk too much. Is it right that others should pay for treatment that might not have been necessary if the patient had not drunk so much for so long?

Dependence on alcohol can lead a person to drink alone and to lose their self-respect.

Drinking alcohol, like taking other drugs, can become a habit that is hard to break. People with alcohol dependence, or alcoholism, find it almost impossible to stop drinking. They have a drink, then another, and continue drinking until they pass out or fall asleep. And then, waking up with a terrible hangover, they start drinking again.

The disease of alcoholism

For many years, people thought alcoholism was a shameful problem suffered by people who had no willpower. Because of this, friends and relatives tried to hide the person's drinking from others. Nowadays, doctors consider alcoholism to be a disease, linked to a person's psychological and physical dependence on alcohol.

Exactly what causes alcoholism is still a mystery, but some people are more likely to develop it than others. Medical studies show that some families have a history of alcohol problems generally. This suggests that alcoholism might be linked to a person's genes.

Facing facts

Even though alcoholism is considered a disease, people should not continue to drink heavily and then wait for treatment if the disease develops. Many people with alcoholism do not realize or accept that they have a problem; they think alcoholism is something that affects other people. They forget that the disease develops slowly and often without the person noticing it. If they or their friends do not recognize some of the warning signs (see panel), then it can become very serious.

Alcohol becomes a way of life for people with a serious dependence. They build their day around drinking, ignoring or forgetting about their other activities and responsibilities. If they continue drinking they risk losing their job, failing at school or wrecking their relationships. They may also become aggressive and violent.

Alcohol dependence can develop in people of all ages. Teenagers can become dependent on alcohol as well as adults.

WARNING SIGNS

Alcoholism takes time to develop, but a number of signs may warn of a drinking problem that could develop into alcohol dependence, or alcoholism. The US National Institute on Alcohol Abuse and Alcoholism lists these for young people. On their own, most would be considered normal for people going through adolescence. However, a combination of signs – or if any of them flares up suddenly or violently – might be a clue to a real problem.

● *Mood changes: flare-ups of temper and irritability.*

● *School problems: low marks, poor attendance or getting into trouble.*

● *Rebelling against family rules.*

● *Changing friends and not introducing new friends to the family.*

● *A 'nothing matters' attitude: sloppy appearance, a lack of involvement in former interests and low energy.*

● *Physical or mental problems: memory lapses, poor concentration, bloodshot eyes, lack of co-ordination or slurred speech.*

Fans still lay tributes at the Paris grave of American rock star Jim Morrison, who died in 1971 after many years of heavy drinking.

" Basically, taking a hip flask and that sort of stuff to school to get through the day and just to deal with life. It sort of became a social dependence I guess. Yeah, drinking half a bottle of whisky a day just getting through each day... At boarding school... in the house, in class. I've always had a problem with anything I've enjoyed, I always go all out and when I found alcohol and I did enjoy it, yeah, I did go all out, and drink as much as I could get my hands on whenever I could. "

Australian teenager describing how his alcohol dependence began at the age of 12.

Some heavy drinkers, including young people, find themselves out of work and homeless because of their problems with alcohol.

THE DTs

The sight of an addict suffering because he or she cannot get hold of a drug is very disturbing. Someone who is dependent on heroin goes through a very uncomfortable period called 'cold turkey' as the body experiences withdrawal symptoms. Alcohol dependency also leads to unpleasant experiences when the drinker goes without alcohol, and in some ways these are more serious than those linked to heroin.

The medical name for these symptoms is *delirium tremens*, although many people shorten this term to DTs. *Delirium tremens* is a Latin phrase, meaning 'trembling delirium'. It describes the uncontrolled shaking a person experiences, often accompanied by vivid hallucinations. The DTs are very exhausting, leaving the person drained as well as terrified. People suffering from this condition should have emergency medical care – even then, the withdrawal symptoms might be fatal.

Some teenagers think that if they drink – and smoke cigarettes – they will look cool and mature.

Studies from around the world agree that alcohol is by far the most popular drug used by young people. In the US, for example, it is used more often than all illegal drugs combined. Using alcohol is illegal for the young people themselves, yet it is sold openly to those old enough to drink it legally. It is almost impossible to prevent some older people buying it for, or even selling it to, under-age drinkers.

Italy may be one of the world's leading wine producers, but Italian teenagers often avoid drinking alcohol when they enjoy themselves.

Alcohol use among young people has been rising in many countries for decades, and continues to rise. Although schools, youth groups and even alcohol producers themselves have highlighted the risks, the problem is increasing. Why?

The power of persuasion

One of the most powerful forces attracting young people to alcohol – and to other illegal drugs – is peer pressure. Many people feel embarrassed or ashamed to be left out of a new, dangerous activity. Young people often begin drinking because they believe it will give them a cool image. The teenage years are a time for learning how to accept responsibilities and to make sensible judgements. Many teenagers find it hard to refuse alcohol, and if they do begin drinking, they lack the experience to understand when alcohol clouds their judgement.

The results can be tragic. In 2001, the US National Highway Traffic Safety Administration reported 3,594 youths between the ages of 15 and 20 killed in car crashes in which somebody had been drinking. The police test for alcohol at the scene of traffic accidents, but there are many other types of fatal accident where alcohol is involved. At least as many children probably died from these other causes, which include drowning, burning, suicide and alcohol poisoning.

ALCOHOL FACT

One survey found that more than a quarter of boys aged 9–10 and a third of those a year older reported drinking alcohol at least once in the previous week, normally at home.

" In our city, teens drink for one reason: there is nothing else to do. It's like it's their only way to have some fun. Every city should take care of their young people as much as possible by offering them more activities. "

Seventeen-year-old boy, quoted in New Brunswick Student Drug Use Survey, 2002

A Scottish youth holds two bottles of high-strength wine as he poses for a passing photographer.

ALCOHOL FACT

Thirty per cent of American children aged 10 to 12 report that they have received a lot of pressure from their classmates to drink beer.

(The Weekly Reader National Survey on Drugs and Alcohol, Field Publications, Spring 1995)

Changing times

The UK Office for National Statistics has followed trends in drinking alcohol and other activities for many decades. Their results prove that alcohol use has increased dramatically among young people. Before about 1950, people aged 18–24 drank less alcohol than any other adult age group in Great Britain. During the 1950s, teenagers began drinking, but most gathered in coffee bars rather than pubs and bars. It was only in the 1960s that young people began going to bars regularly, signalling a sudden rise in alcohol use among that group. By the 1980s, the 18–24 age group had reversed the position of 30 years earlier – they had become the adult group that drank more alcohol than any other.

Champagne is part of the popular high-class image of young women who attend the races at Ascot in England.

SEARCHING QUESTION

Imagine you have just arrived at a party where most of the young people, including some of your friends, are drinking. They urge you to join them but you don't want to drink any alcohol. Can you think of a way to refuse their offer without making them – or you – feel embarrassed?

Eye-catching labels make bottles of alcopop look like fizzy drinks on the shelves in shops.

Even secure young people find the whole issue of alcohol complicated. On one hand, adults warn about the serious problems relating to alcohol. On the other, advertisements and TV commercials show people having a great time with alcohol. Which is the true story, and how can people make up their own minds?

Controlling advertisements

Learning to decode the mixed messages we receive from different sections of society is an important part of growing up. Most adults can make up their minds without too much persuasion from friends or from the world of advertising. Younger people have had less experience, and find these decisions harder to make.

As a result, most countries have strict guidelines about how alcohol can be advertised. In some countries, such as the US, a TV commercial cannot show people putting a glass or bottle of alcohol to their lips. In the UK, the restrictions are a bit looser. Here, a commercial cannot make it seem that drinking alcohol is the only reason a group of happy people is having a good time. Nearly everywhere, alcohol advertising is forbidden in children's magazines or at times of the day when young people are most likely to be watching TV.

ALCOHOL FACT

In the US, junior/middle and senior high school students drink 35 per cent of all wine coolers and 1.1 billion cans of beer.
From *"Youth and Alcohol: A National Survey. Drinking Habits, Access, Attitudes, and Knowledge"*, Washington, DC, June 1991.

Targeting young drinkers

Drinks called alcopops mask the taste of alcohol with sweet or fruity flavours. It is very easy to drink several without realizing how strong they are. They are often far stronger than beer.

The youth advertising message seems to be effective, even on those who are too young to drink alcohol legally. A Scottish survey in 2003 found that 13-year-old boys were as likely to drink alcopops as beer, wine or cider. A similar survey in Wales found that parents were giving children alcopops at parties and barbecues.

Student bars are popular meeting places for young people at college or university.

SEARCHING QUESTION

Many parents, police officers and alcohol counsellors worry that advertising alcoholic drinks encourages people – especially young people – to drink too much and too early in their lives. Some of them would like to see alcohol advertising more strictly controlled or even banned. What do you think?

A police officer uses a breathalyser to measure the amount of alcohol in a driver's body.

Imagine how frightening it would be to face a drunken person waving a deadly weapon. When someone who has drunk too much drives a car, they turn it into a lethal weapon. Even at very low speeds, a car can severely injure or kill people – pedestrians or passengers. That possibility makes driving a big responsibility. Drivers need to make split-second decisions. Even the smallest amount of alcohol in the blood can affect their ability to do this.

Drunken people often become loud and violent and occasionally wave deadly weapons. Others, especially young people who have adolescent troubles, can feel overwhelmed by their worries and harm themselves. Alcohol makes them forget how to address these anxieties with common sense and so makes them worse. This can be dangerous for young drinkers and for those around them.

SAFETY TIPS

The US campaigning group Mothers Against Drunk Driving (MADD) publicizes the dangers of drinking alcohol and driving. Often children cannot refuse a ride from an adult (sometimes a loved one) – who has had too much alcohol to drive a car safely. The organization offers children the following advice, which could save a life.

ALWAYS
Sit in the back seat.

Buckle up tight.

Put all stuff on the floor.

Don't bother the driver – just sit quietly.

Tell a trusted grown-up immediately about any unsafe ride.

Deadly combination

People who have drunk alcohol lose co-ordination and take dangerous risks – a deadly combination. In July 2000, a team of Swedish doctors published the results of a five-year survey of the link between alcohol and accidental deaths. They found that 29 per cent of all accidental deaths in Sweden were linked to alcohol and estimated that the figure could be as high as 44 per cent in countries, such as the UK and Australia, where the laws are less tough.

These results are supported by alcohol experts in other countries. On 14 July 2000, Sue Boon, assistant director of Alcohol Concern, said that alcohol played a part in 65 per cent of UK suicide attempts. She also said that eight out of 10 people treated at hospital accident and emergency departments at peak times have had an accident linked with alcohol.

A roadside bunch of flowers marks the site of a fatal car accident.

ALARM BELLS

The US-based National Institute on Alcohol Abuse and Alcoholism (NIAAA) publishes evidence about the effects of alcohol on young people and on society generally. The following facts were published in the spring of 2003.

● *The rate of alcohol–related traffic crashes is more than twice as great for drivers aged 16–20 than for drivers aged 21 and older.*

● *Underage alcohol use is more likely to kill young people than all illegal drugs combined.*

● *Alcohol use combines stress and depression to contribute to suicide, the third biggest cause of death among people aged between 14 and 25.*

● *Alcohol lessens a person's ability to make sensible judgements, which means that young men and women may have high-risk sex (sex with more than one partner and not using a condom). This puts people at risk of becoming pregnant or of developing a sexually transmitted disease, including HIV/AIDS. Studies indicate that the risk of this behaviour increases with the amount a person drinks.*

Iraqi men drink tea at a café. Most Iraqis belong to the Islamic faith, which bans the use of alcohol.

For thousands of years, families, schools, religious groups and countries have tried to set some limits on the use and availability of alcohol. Some limits are aimed at a particular group, mainly the young, who risk most by drinking. Other limits have been designed to stop everyone from drinking because of the problems alcohol causes society as a whole.

Underage drinking

Some Islamic countries, such as Saudi Arabia, ban alcohol completely because it is against their religion. Most countries set their strictest limits for young people to prevent underage drinking. Australians under 18 cannot buy or drink alcohol legally.

In the UK, the 1964 Licensing Act gives more detailed guidelines. People under 14 cannot enter most pubs but those who are 16 and over can have relatively low-alcohol drinks such as beer or cider with a meal in a pub or restaurant, provided they are with an adult. Otherwise, the rule is the same as in Australia.

The US has changed its drinking laws many times. Until 1984, each state decided its own laws. Then, the federal government passed the National Minimum Drinking Age Act, which required all states to raise the age for buying and drinking alcohol in public to 21. Although the act does not ban those aged 18–21 from drinking, it prevents them from doing so in most cases.

ALCOHOL FACTS

● *Drinking increases with age: 14 per cent of 12–13 year-olds, 33 per cent of 14–15 year-olds and 62 per cent of 16–17 year-olds had drunk alcohol in the last week.*

● *The number of young people drinking alcohol in the last week has risen from 21 per cent of 11–15 year-olds in 1999 to 25 per cent in 2003. This has reversed the previous downward trend from 27 per cent in 1996 to 21 per cent in 1998.*
(Institute of Alcohol Studies, UK.)

An underage drinker hides his alcohol in a paper bag. Without guidance, young people find it hard to know their own drinking limits.

SEARCHING QUESTION

Many people believe that tough punishments act as a deterrent. In other words, knowing that the punishment for an action will be severe, a person will probably choose not to do it. Many campaigners believe that the punishments for drunk-driving are not serious enough to be a deterrent. Can you think of a punishment that would stop more people from starting a car after they have had a drink?

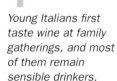

Young Italians first taste wine at family gatherings, and most of them remain sensible drinkers.

GOING EASY IN ITALY

Italians drink roughly the same amount of alcohol per person as people in countries such as the UK and the US, but Italy has fewer social problems linked to alcohol – such as violence and public drunkenness. Italians are brought up to know about wine and other alcoholic drinks. This means that most of them have their first drink in a family setting, where they learn about the dangers of drinking too much. As a result, teenagers consider alcohol as just one of the things that goes with meeting other people – never the only reason people get together in the first place.

Young and old Italians frown on drinking too much, especially in public. Doctor Enrico Tempesta, an Italian government scientist studying alcohol and youth, explains: "Here, children and teenagers disapprove and tend to exclude from their circle a contemporary who gets drunk".

Police officers destroy barrels of rum in San Francisco during Prohibition, the period during which the US banned alcoholic drinks.

Banning alcohol

From the middle of the 19th century, many Americans – especially women – were concerned about alcohol and its effects on the country. Many men regularly went to saloons, spent their wages on drink and often left their families with little money to live on. Drinking also affected the economy, with many people missing work, arriving late or trying to work while drunk.

By the beginning of the 20th century, groups favouring prohibition (banning alcohol altogether) in the US, gained support. Similar movements developed in Canada, Finland and the UK. In 1919, the US government amended, or changed, the Constitution so that alcohol was banned across the country. Prohibition remained in force throughout the 1920s, though many Americans found ways of drinking alcohol in speakeasies (secret bars) or through bootleggers (people who imported alcohol illegally).

By the early 1930s, many Americans had tired of Prohibition and believed that individuals, not the government, should be allowed to decide for themselves whether or not to drink alcohol. In 1933, the Constitution was changed again, making it legal once more to sell, buy and drink alcohol in the US.

SEARCHING QUESTION
Some Americans argue that the drinking age should be lowered in the US. But some experts in the UK and other countries want to raise their drinking age to 21. What do you think?

Teenage drinking can lead to tiredness and poor performance at school.

Teachers and others in the education system need to have a common policy on how to keep their schools free of alcohol, and how to ensure that alcohol drunk away from school does not disrupt other children's chances to learn.

In nearly every country, school-age children are too young to drink alcohol legally, but calling the police into school every time a child is suspected of drinking would be very disruptive. Like parents, school staff have a duty to look after young people. That duty sometimes calls for a delicate balance – disciplining drinkers while at the same time offering positive alternatives to having alcohol.

Students at West Covina High School in Los Angeles carry a coffin into the school gym. This is part of a course which explains to teenagers that someone is killed in an alcohol-related car crash every 15 minutes. The students role play the deaths of four teenagers in the space of an hour. They write obituaries and re-enact failed attempts to save the teenagers' lives.

Zero tolerance

One of the most dramatic ways of dealing with alcohol in schools is to be as strict as possible once someone has broken the school rules about drinking alcohol.

Many schools in the US and in other countries operate a zero-tolerance policy towards alcohol. Students know that they won't simply receive a warning when they are caught the first time – they will face the stiffest penalty imposed by the school, which could be expulsion.

People in favour of zero-tolerance policies argue that schools benefit immediately and that children understand such schemes because they know where they stand at all times.

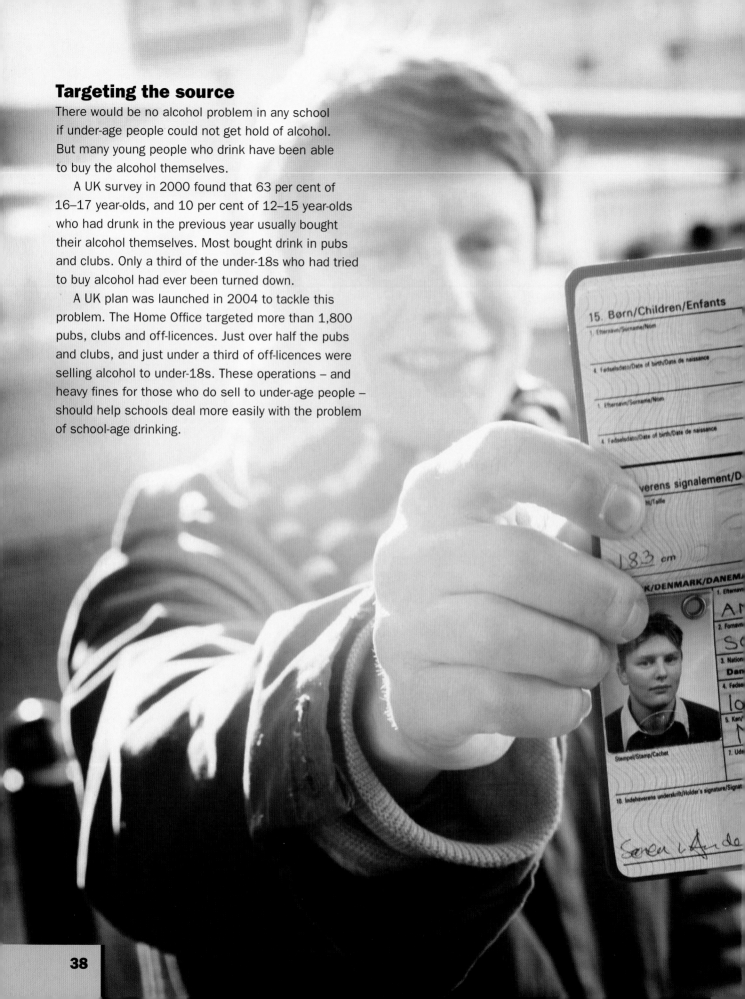

Targeting the source

There would be no alcohol problem in any school if under-age people could not get hold of alcohol. But many young people who drink have been able to buy the alcohol themselves.

A UK survey in 2000 found that 63 per cent of 16–17 year-olds, and 10 per cent of 12–15 year-olds who had drunk in the previous year usually bought their alcohol themselves. Most bought drink in pubs and clubs. Only a third of the under-18s who had tried to buy alcohol had ever been turned down.

A UK plan was launched in 2004 to tackle this problem. The Home Office targeted more than 1,800 pubs, clubs and off-licences. Just over half the pubs and clubs, and just under a third of off-licences were selling alcohol to under-18s. These operations – and heavy fines for those who do sell to under-age people – should help schools deal more easily with the problem of school-age drinking.

> **"** *Some pupils come into school drunk or with hangovers. It has quite a devastating effect. They come into school with a hangover, they've got a headache, they want to sleep, they can't concentrate... It sometimes leads to behaviour that has a knock-on effect on the rest of the group so their learning is affected.* **"**

A headteacher in the UK, recorded in a BBC News Survey 2004

Russian girls drink beer in a Moscow park, like more and more teenagers in other parts of the world.

SEARCHING QUESTION

Some people argue that a zero-tolerance approach to alcohol, drugs and other problems is unfair because it does not give pupils a chance to improve their behaviour. Also, children might be wrongly accused or set up by fellow pupils. Do you think these concerns are enough to abandon such schemes or do you think schools need a firm and clear-cut policy on dealing with alcohol and other substances?

Many young people find it easier to deal with their alcohol problems in discussion groups or counselling sessions.

Someone who has a problem with alcohol may feel very lonely. That problem can come from their own drinking or from the sadness and stress of having a family member who drinks too much. A good way of approaching it is to work outwards. Young people who feel comfortable in their own home should turn to older family members.

Looking for advice

Beyond the family many individuals and groups can offer help and advice. Schools and youth groups can point a young person in the direction of trained counsellors who are experts in helping people of all ages come to terms with alcohol.

Some national and international alcohol organizations are listed at the end of this book, along with some recommended books on the subject. More local organizations are listed in the telephone directory under the headings alcohol, alcohol awareness and alcohol concerns. Key in similar phrases, along with the nearest town or city, to search the Internet for websites and addresses of organizations.

Family matters

Problem drinking by young people spills over into the family as a whole – causing rows and endangering relationships between parents and children, and brothers and sisters. Some problems can be traced back to the parents themselves. Parents' attitudes and habits relating to alcohol shape much of their children's behaviour.

Parents with alcohol problems make their children suffer. Such children often do badly at school, and have emotional and psychological problems. These children may find it hard to move into adulthood, keep friendships and pull away from the family. Some begin drinking heavily themselves, storing up troubles for the next generation.

AN INSIDER'S STORY

Jenny (not her real name), from the city of Bath in the west of England, is 18. Her story is typical of people who don't realize they have a serious drink problem.

"I started drinking cider and lager when I was 14. Older friends would buy me and my friends a few cans or tall bottles. We'd spend Friday and Saturday evening drinking, either at the far end of the park or at someone's house if their parents were out. It was good for a laugh, but then I started to feel I wanted to drink more, and more often."

Shoplifting

"I would tell my parents that I was at a sleepover or party and then start drinking at lunchtime on Saturday. Then I began to skip school and hang out with some older kids who also liked a drink. Sometimes I shoplifted drink if I had no money. Other times I would go into the pub with the older ones – only if it was crowded and the staff didn't notice me. I started to have real problems at school and most of my older friends – even the ones I had started drinking with – dropped me. At that time I thought, 'No way do I have a drink problem. It's not vodka or even wine with me – just lager and cider and maybe the odd alcopop.''

> **" I would tell my parents that I was at a sleepover or party and then start drinking at lunchtime on Saturday. "**

Getting help

"The headteacher at my school finally cornered me. She told me to face facts – not aggressively or threatening me with anything. Just to face facts, and see where my life was leading. I argued a bit, trying to defend myself, but eventually I got the nerve to phone an alcohol advisory centre. They were great – no hassles, just good at listening. I started popping in for chats, and they showed me how I'd start to enjoy life much more if I stayed sober. That came as a shock, 'What me? An alcoholic?' I thought. But it was worth listening. I took their advice and have stopped drinking. I even told some of my older friends about it, just after I took the decision. They were great and they've been a real support for me over the first few months. I've even joined a drama group – it helps me let off steam if I feel wound up."

The headteacher at my school finally cornered me. She told me to face facts.

Young people can laugh, share secrets and have a good time without needing to drink alcohol.

ABV an abbreviation of Alcohol By Volume, showing how much of a drink is made up of pure alcohol. The higher the number, the stronger the drink

adolescence the period in a person's teenage years marking the change from childhood to adulthood

alcoholism a physical and psychological dependence on alcohol

alcohol poisoning an overdose of alcohol at one time that puts a strain on one or more parts of the body

binge drinking drinking a lot at one time

blitz a sudden attack

bloodshot (of the eyes) appearing red and showing small blood vessels

cirrhosis an alcohol-related disease of the liver caused by a build-up of scar tissue

compound a chemical mixture of two or more substances

concentration the amount of a particular substance found in a mixture

constitution a written document spelling out how a country is governed

contemporary a person about the same as age as yourself

culture the customs and way of life of a country

dilute to add another substance to a mixture (usually a liquid) to lessen the concentration of something else

distillation a process of producing strong alcoholic drinks by boiling away a liquid that contains alcohol to get rid of some of the other ingredients

fatal causing death

fermentation a natural way of producing alcoholic drinks (such as wine) by leaving a juice so that the sugar turns into alcohol

genes the basic chemical code of human beings, which determines how they will develop

hallucination an imaginary vision caused by a high fever or a drug

hangover an unpleasant feeling, including dry mouth, headache and upset stomach, experienced the day after drinking a lot of alcohol

high blood pressure a medical condition in which a person's blood pressure is persistently higher than normal

HIV/AIDS an abbreviation of Human Immunodeficiency Virus, which can cause a deadly condition called Acquired Immune Deficiency Syndrome

import to bring in from another country

insecure lacking in confidence

insurance a type of payment that provides money in an accident or emergency

Islamic concerning the Muslim religion, based on the teachings of the Prophet Muhammad

licensing giving legal permission to sell something such as alcohol

peer pressure powerful persuasion from similar-aged friends to do something

prescription drugs medicines that a doctor decides are necessary to treat an illness

prohibition a complete ban on a particular action (from the word "prohibit", or forbid)

psychological to do with the mind

reaction a chemical change

sexually-transmitted disease an illness passed on from one person to another through sexual activity

stimulant a drug that makes people feel more alert

ulcer a hole in the stomach lining

vineyard an area where grape vines are grown

withdrawal symptoms the physical and psychological changes in a person who stops taking a drug after becoming dependent on it

Books

When Someone You Love Abuses Alcohol or Drugs – A Guide for Kids. J. J. Crist (editor). (Wellness Institute, Stevens Point, Wisconsin, 2003)

Alcohol (Talking Points series). E. Hawton. (Hodder Wayland, 1998)

Alcofacts: A Guide to Sensible Drinking. Health Promotion Wales. (Cardiff, 1997)

Just Say No: Talking with Kids About Drugs and Alcohol. C. Kuhn, S. Swartzwelder and W. Wilson. (W. W. Norton & Co, Ltd, 2002)

The Big Deal about Alcohol: What Teens Need to Know about Drinking (Issues in Focus series). M. McClellan. (Enslow Publishers, Berkeley Heights, NJ, 2005)

Drugs (Wise Guides series). A. Naik. (Hodder Children's Books, 1997)

Drinking Alcohol (Choices and Decisions series). P. Saunders. and S. Myers. (Franklin Watts, 2004)

Websites

Al-Anon and Alateen
www.Al-Anon-Alateen.org/
Offers advice and practical steps for young people whose families or friends are affected by alcohol abuse.

The Cool Spot
www.thecoolspot.org/
A website aimed squarely at young people's concerns about alcohol, with interactive quizzes, polls and all sorts of information about alcohol and how to say no.

Drug Smart Z Card
http://www.youth.nsw.gov.au/__data/page/52/ZDrugsSmart2005web150a.pdf
An Australian site full of information about alcohol and other drugs, with detailed information and useful links.

The Site
www.thesite.org
A UK youth-based site full of information about alcohol and other drugs, with the latest information about changing UK alcohol laws and how they affect young people.

Talk4Teens
www.talk4teens.co.uk
A UK website covering the most important teen health issues, including a detailed and useful section on alcohol.